101 Tips On How To Be A Bouncer:

Techniques to Handle Situations Without Violence

Darren Lee

DISCLAIMER

The material in this publication is of a general nature, and neither purports nor intends to be advice. This publication is sold with the understanding that neither the author, nor publisher is engaged in rendering legal, or other professional service. If legal advice or other expert assistance is required, the services of a competent professional person in your legal jurisdiction should be sought. The author and publisher expressly disclaim all and any liability to any person, whether a purchaser of this publication or not, in respect of anything and of the consequences done or omitted to be done by any such person in reliance, whether whole or partial, upon the whole or any part of the contents of this publication.

DEDICATION

To the Annoying, Intoxicated Patrons of the world, without whom none of this would have been possible.

CONTENTS

ACKNOWLEDGMENTS

I wish to express my profound thank you to a very special bunch of people who ran a communication course I completed many years ago, which sparked my continuing quest to try and handle anything with communication and improve my understanding of people. The emphasis of this course on 'intention' and using the appropriate emotion for the situation, both are constant themes throughout this book, has changed my whole approach not only to crowd control but life in general. You know who you are and if the reader wishes to know more about this group, please fire off an email to Linda at Intentionunleashed@gmail.com

To my brother and dad who encouraged me to follow my entrepreneurial spirit outside of the safety of a 9 to 5 job and do what I love.

To the countless crowd controllers who gave up their pet techniques for the benefit of the reader and patiently helped me through a grueling review process of which techniques were the most effective. In particular, Nathan James, Big Willie, Silver Fox, Whitey, Shane Pollard, Matt Roles and veteran police officer Simon Williams, your contribution is very much appreciated.

A special thank you also goes to fellow author, Ron Steele, who worked with me in the review stages of the project when I needed some experienced insight.

i

PREFACE

When I tell people about my background as a crowd controller I usually get a whole range of mixed reactions ranging from, "What, a bouncer?" to "Are you serious?" or "But you seem so nice." I have to laugh when I get these reactions because I suppose I do not fit the stereotype of a seven-foot, tattoo-covered, gym-junkie, arrogant "bouncer." For you see, my background is somewhat different to what you would expect from the average "bouncer."

Firstly, I have worked as a dispute resolution lawyer for many years in a nice building, with a nice secretary and a nice coffee machine. Does this disqualify me from having the necessary background to write this book? Has this book-smart dude ever even worked in a club outside of his cozy office, you ask? I'll let you decide whether you find the techniques herein practical and workable in the field, but for now I assure you I have spent more than enough time actually in the field to know what works. I have been involved in the crowd control industry on and off now for over 10 years and have regularly worked at many major concert venues, bars, clubs, private parties, immigration detention centres, mining camps, community security patrols, hospitals, shopping centres, etc. You name it, I've done it!

Since entering security, my approach has significantly changed for what I believe is the better and my background as a lawyer involved in countless grueling disputes and negotiations has considerably influenced the way I deal with oppositional situations. This book is the culmination of many years of work in attempting to codify the techniques I have found most workable in handling situations in the crowd control environment without resorting to violence. Although intended for crowd controllers, there is little doubt that nightclub managers, bar tenders, and event organizers will find these tips valuable in their security supervision and planning role.

When people think of a bouncer it is usually of an arrogant brute with no IQ who loves violence and throwing people head first into trash bins. Generally this could be referred to as an Old School bouncer and in this day and age where most clubs have 'no hit' policies and you could lose your security license or be sued for overstepping the mark of what is reasonable force even slightly, I have found these old school bouncers do not last very long in the industry.

Despite the virtual extinction of Old School bouncers in today's nightlife, much to my surprise, very little has been written for bouncers on how to handle situations without violence, so called New School techniques. The fact is, you may have a very extensive martial arts and gym record but if you cannot communicate with people and use your mind to handle situations, you are putting yourself and others at risk by being in this industry.

My hope with this book is that it will encourage you into a new approach to crowd control and keep you to engaging in as little violence as possible. This book is not intended to be a definitive work on the new school techniques of crowd control but rather, is a work in progress to be updated in later editions as techniques are found which are more workable. In the meantime, I hope you enjoy this book and are able to find some helpful tips you are able to make your own.

"Whoever ceases to be a student has never been a student." George Iles

INTRODUCTION

The 3 rules of crowd control are:

"1. Never underestimate your opponent. Expect the unexpected;

2. Take it outside. Don't ever start something in the bar unless it's absolutely necessary; and

3. Be nice until it's time not to be nice."

These rules were stated by head of security, James Dalton, played by Patrick Swayze in the movie Road House (1989), one of my all-time favorite movies and one I recommend to anybody working in nightclub security. This text seeks to expand on these rules and provide you with a whole arsenal of techniques you can use before, in the words of Dalton, "It's time not to be nice."

The themes contained in this text can be summarized into roughly the following 20 Golden Rules which can be used to formulate your own techniques:

1. Act with intention, not anger

2. Be proactive and anticipate situations

3. Be nice until it's time not to be nice

4. Communicate with and listen to people

5. Use the good guy/bad guy approach

6. Use warnings to increase your bargaining power

7. Use the win/win tactic by taking a hard line and then relaxing it

8. Use canned routines for ID Checks, Intoxication tests and Evictions

9. Maintain an authoritative presence

10. 'Ghost' abuse and do not let it affect you

11. Agree with people to get them onside

12. Never put somebody into a fight or flight situation

13. Stop them at the door

14. Use your environment

15. Work as a team and back up your fellow crowd controller's call

16. Do not show fear

17. Be in present time and leave your troubles at the door

18. Know your limits

19. Know the law and rules of the venue

20. Do not fight your own battles if you can avoid it

Because of this text's emphasis on new school techniques, I have chosen not to refer to venue security professionals as 'bouncers' which has an old school vibe about it, but rather have used the term 'crowd controllers', which is the preferred term in Australia and many other countries. The role of the crowd controller is essentially to ensure the liquor licensing laws are being followed, to help the venue make money by letting in the appropriate clientele and to help the patrons have a good time without feeling intimidated. Bouncers still very much exist in the nightlife scene, but should be brought in as last resort when the crowd controllers fail.

Now, what to call the intoxicated people who constantly hurl abuse and cause us problems throughout the night. Well, let me first say that I have a firm belief that people are basically good and well intentioned and regardless of how they may act at times, they generally mean well and are just trying to have a fun night out. We all like to have a drink out now and again, but there comes a point when people under the influence of drugs and alcohol just take it too far. Throughout years of experience as a crowd controller, I have genuinely found it helpful to remember that these people deep down are basically good and to try and bring out the best in them, in the hope that it will overcome their temporary irrational state.

But again, what to call these people? Well, here we are not talking about the person in their natural, rational state, but rather in their wild, primitive, beastly, ghastly state of intoxicated irrationality. An appropriate name in my view would be **Annoying Intoxicated Patron** or **AIP** as they do seem to bear an extraordinary resemblance at times to their primitive ape cousins.

Now before we begin, I would suggest that the best way to read this book is to just scan through it and find something with which you agree, and then find another tip with which you agree. Nobody expects you to agree with everything or to use it all but if you learn just one useful new idea or tactic for your crowd controller role then my effort in putting together this text will have been worthwhile.

1 THE FRONT DOOR

The front door is where it all happens. This is easily the most dangerous place in the venue and usually where the most experienced crowd controller, the head doorman, spends most of the night. As a fellow crowd controller, Oscar, once said, "every night is a hustle." This is because you must be able to read people in a split second and convince them to follow your directions, while all the time trying to talk down aggressors, being hit on continuously by girls in an attempt to distract you, playing cat and mouse with people trying to sneak in, and all the while remain cool with a smile on your face.

For anybody who thinks all a doorman does is stand around chatting to girls all night and pushing people around, I challenge them to work for just one night on the door and see how long it takes before they snap! To be a successful doorman you must have a whole range of skills including being a good bullsh!t artist, counselor, comedian, actor, martial artist, negotiator, public speaker, hustler, baby-sitter, judge and jury. Above all else, you must have gigantic, thundering balls because you will not last two minutes in this industry otherwise. But you'll find all that out soon enough. Let's get into the action!

TIP #1

The entrance to the venue is your zone. It is very important that you maintain authority over who comes into the venue as if the wrong people are allowed inside the result can be disastrous later in the night. Some security teams even have a custom that, "Whoever lets them in gets them out" to encourage the front door to be run tightly and ensure only the appropriate clientele get inside.

The front door should be kept clear at all times, with a clear distinction between the entrance and exit. If the venue does not already have one, they should be encouraged to install a traditional velvet rope that you can use to control the line and delay patrons from coming inside. This increases the time you have to assess patrons for dress code, intoxication levels and general demeanor. If you do not control the entrance to the venue, it can cause difficulties later on because people will try and rush past, you will have difficulty checking IDs, you will be more easily distracted by people trying to keep you occupied in conversation so their more intoxicated friend can sneak in, there will not be a clear exit pathway in the case of an eviction during the night, and so on.

TIP #2

Greet everyone who enters the venue like they are VIPs and, as the old saying goes, "treat others as you would expect to be treated." If you go out of your way to get people on your side before they enter the venue, this will go a long way towards helping you later in the night. I make it a regular practice to open the door for every patron that enters and greet them like they are movie stars. Later on in the night when I am patrolling the venue, people often smile at and come and talk to me because they were so flattered by my gentlemanly approach on the door. When it comes time for evictions and requests that people keep their behavior under control, etc. do not underestimate the power achieved early in the night of getting the unruly patron and their friends and bystanders on your side.

Greeting people at the door also has value as an intoxication/potential aggravation test. If you greet somebody at the door and they do not respond to you, straight away ask them again how their night is going. If they react well, are friendly and do not appear intoxicated, then wish them a pleasant night in the venue. However, if they react negatively towards you, tell them up front that it is your job to get friendly people with good manners as patrons and if they are rude to you, then the chances of them being rude to the staff are pretty high, so they will not be coming into the venue that night. If they protest, you can either stick to your guns and not let them in or **relax your hard line** and say that you will let them in on the condition that they cool off for half an hour/have some water or food and then come back (win/win). This tactic usually works very well now that you have **gained leverage** over them. You have come to know them better and often they will be overly nice to you during the night and in future because you *helped them out* by letting them in.

TIP #3

Before we get into more detail on the tactics used to refuse people entry at the door, deal with abuse and conduct evictions, I want to emphasize an underlying principle which is absolutely crucial to preventing a situation from escalating. This principle is to act with **INTENTION WITHOUT RESERVATION**. Think of this as your secret Jedi power. When you verbally or physically command an action with intention and no reservations, the person you are directing will have no choice but to go along with it. A lot could be said about why this principle works (and if you contact my friend, Linda on Intentionunleashed@gmail.com she will be more than pleased to direct you to a course that will allow you to truly harness your intention) but for now just apply it and see for yourself that it does work.

Throughout this book I have continuously underlined the word 'intention' so it begins to sink in. By the end of this book you will be sick of reading the word, but you won't forget it!

Example - Think of when you were a child and your mother demanded you pick up your toys or clean your room. You may have argued, kicked the cat and slammed your door, but you DID CLEAN THE ROOM! Your mother simply acted with intention which pierced through all your irrationality and got you to clean the room.

AIPs have an uncanny ability to sense even the slightest doubt in your mind that you can handle the situation and will use this against you every chance they get. Acting with intention most certainly does not mean being rude as your wording should always be fair and reasonable, but it does mean being effective and sticking to your guns.

Countless times I have seen professional crowd controllers removing people twice their size just because they made the decision to evict them and followed it through without any reservations.

If you glare at somebody or show any other overt signs of aggression, they will match this by showing you aggression. Instead, you must learn to act with intention and not react to the AIP's abuse. When they realize that this is not a negotiation and you mean business, they will often drop their anger against you, because it is having no effect, and will comply with your request the way a child would when picking up their toys after an initial tantrum.

TIP #4

Use canned routines to refuse for intoxication. The following are examples of two highly successful routines included here courtesy of a veteran crowd controller friend of mine, Nathan James. I refer to them as 'canned' routines because they usually have little variation and can be performed over and over again without thinking. As you will see, these canned routines contain a combination of humor, delay tactics to increase your time to assess the person and deflecting the attention off yourself with use of the good guy/bad guy approach placing the law as the bad guy.

CANNED ROUTINE 1 (The Police Officer)

1. You assess that the person appears too intoxicated to enter the venue and so greet them and ask, "How many drinks have you had tonight?"

2. They will usually lie and tell you less drinks than they have had so ask, "How long ago did you start and when was the last drink?"

3. Compare their answer to the prescribed legal driving limit in your State and tell them they are over the legal driving limit. They will then usually respond with, "That's ok, I am not driving."

4. You then pull out your standard line of, "I understand that, sir, but unfortunately under [the law of your State], if someone is showing signs of intoxication we are legally obligated to refuse them entry. As we have just established, you are near or over the legal limit for driving and so are pretty close to the stage of showing **signs of intoxication**. If I let you in, I am risking a personal fine, as well as a fine for anybody who serves you along with the venue manager and the venue itself (place the law as the bad guy to deflect the attention off you). As you can imagine, that adds up to a lot of fines, so if you were in my position, would you let yourself in?"

5. a) If they say, "probably not," then you can respond with, "Thank you, sir, I am glad you understand. If you sober up and come back in an hour or so, I'll see how you are and if you are ok to come in" (relax the hard line now that you have gained leverage over them).

b) If they say, "Yes I would," which is the most common response, then run through the following routine with them, "Ok sir, can you do one last thing for me? Just stand on one leg without holding anything, and hold it up for a while so I can check your balance. Then when I ask you to switch it, switch to the other leg for me. And don't worry I'll be doing it with you, so I am not trying to make you look bad or anything."

Then stand on one leg yourself, and they will usually stumble at this point.

Then respond with, "Ok, sir, well I don't feel comfortable risking a fine by letting you on the premises at the moment, so I am sorry but I have to say 'no' to you at this time. If you can go get some food, maybe some water, and take a bit of time to sober up you can come back in about an hour and I'll see if you are better then."

If they ask you whether they can definitely come back at that time, do not commit to an answer, just say you will need to reassess the situation then and with <u>intention</u> guide them out of the line and call up the next group for ID checks. The other people in the line will then use peer pressure to stop the AIP from hanging around holding up the line as they persist trying to get in.

CANNED ROUTINE 2 (The Comedian)

1. If you suspect somebody is too intoxicated to enter, ask to see their ID and then stall them by saying, "Happy birthday."

2. When they laugh and look confused say, "Am I too early or too late?"

3. As they fumble around trying to figure out when their birthday is, you can delay them even further by asking, "What are you doing for your actual birthday?"

4. If you have assessed by now that they are articulate enough to enter the premises, then just laugh and, if it is a guy, shake their hand and wish them a good night or if it is a girl, pretend to be upset that

6

you are not invited to her big birthday party and get a hug from her. This playful little routine helps to end off your test on a happy note, so the person doesn't feel like they have just been interrogated, which can set a bad vibe for the remainder of the night. Once you have done this routine with them, people will also remember you on future nights and automatically treat you nicely because you were the funny birthday bouncer, etc.

5. If the AIP starts getting impatient at this point, doesn't play along and appears to be struggling with their thought process, then refuse them entry on the ground that they are showing signs of intoxication, and merge into the routine of how the law will not let them in, etc. as in routine 1 above.

CANNED ROUTINE 3 (The Trickster)

The following routine has been contributed by crowd controller friend, Matt Roles, and subtly forces the patron to respond to a tricky question to slow them down and give you a better opportunity to assess their intoxication level.

1. You observe that the person appears intoxicated and greet them with, "Hi guys, how many drinks have you had tonight?"

2. They will invariably respond with, "Umm...a couple."

3. You then ask how many drinks that is, and they clarify their response by saying, "3 or 4," "5 or 6," etc.

4. If you determine at this point that they have had too much to drink, then refuse them entry.

5. However, if they still appear reasonably coherent, but you want to dig further, ask the following trick question: "...and how many is in a couple?" This phrase is deliberately ambiguous encouraging the patron to use their mind, and their response will usually vary depending on their level of intoxication and whether they are already

in an aggressive mood.

6. Your response will vary depending on each of the following situations:

    a)   They repeat the number of drinks they actually had rather than specifically addressing your question (i.e. Giving the correct answer that a couple is 'two'). In this case, just clarify in a fun and non-condescending manner that you are asking how many is in a couple, in the general sense. If they are not intoxicated and not aggressive, they will usually just say the correct answer of "two," laugh with you and then you can let them inside;

    b)   The person states the number of drinks they actually had as in a) above, but becomes aggressive or impatient with you when you clarify that you want to know how many is in a couple generally by saying e.g. "Can I just go in the club?", or "Fine there's TWO!", etc. In this case refuse them entry as, provided you asked the question in a playful, non-condescending manner, they were unreasonably aggressive towards you so you do not want them inside the venue; or

    c)   They give the correct answer of "two" or "three" and laugh with you because they know their initial answer stated they had had more than two or three drinks. In this case, just laugh and say something like, "Get in there you funny buggers" or "Congratulations, you have won the $2 pop quiz," etc. to smooth them over as you let them inside.

I also note that an alternative tricky question for this scenario could have been to ask them to pronounce 'residency' and 'citizenship', which is a favorite of my friend, Big Al, and a crack up to watch drunks try to pronounce.

CANNED ROUTINE 4 (Take 'Em All On)

The following routine was contributed by Silver Fox, who has over twenty years experience in the industry. This routine works well, particularly with large groups of guys (such as a football team or bucks night), in situations where you know they are too intoxicated to enter the venue and are not prepared to spend time 'testing' them.

1. If the group has not yet entered the line of the venue, you should initially refuse them on the ground that the venue does not let in large groups of guys as it is female friendly, or find something wrong with their dress code as explored further in TIPS #5 and 6. As they argue with you, you can soften the blow by asserting that you are doing them a favor by telling them before they enter the line as the 'head doorman' or 'door chick' won't them in.

2. However, if the group has been in line for some time, they will feel an entitlement to enter the venue and so a more tactful approach is required.

As they approach the front of the line, stop the group and ask in a friendly manner, "What are you drinking?" or "What's your drink guys?" The beauty of these questions is that the group is not likely to say a low alcoholic drink because they want to appear masculine to you.

3. Your next response will depend on their answer:

   a) If they say 'beer', and you are working in an up-market venue such as a wine bar, then you can suggest with <u>intention</u> and in a friendly manner, that they go to the venue down the road which has a pint and pizza night, cheap jugs of beer, etc. and move them out of the line as if doing them a favor;

   b) If they say 'bourbon' or another high alcoholic drink, then say something along the lines of how that is a very strong drink and recommend an even more up-market venue for them to go to as you move them out of the line.

4. If the group refuses to leave the line and insists on coming inside, make up an excuse such as, the venue is female friendly and does not let in large groups of guys, or find something wrong with their dress code. After waiting in line for so long, the group will feel an entitlement to enter the venue and protest your refusal to let them in on the ground that your reason for not letting them in should have been communicated prior to them lining up. In this case just ignore them and let it simmer. As the group starts to become aggressive with you, you can then use that aggression as the ground not to let them in and pretend, or actually call the police to encourage them to move on.

TIP #5

Utilize Dress Code to refuse entry. Often rules on dress code are very broad and deliberately vague to allow you room to utilize as a tool to refuse undesirable AIPs entry. If the venue does not already have a dress code posted at the entrance to the venue, encourage them to get one that says roughly the following, so you can refer to it to defer responsibility for the decision to refuse entry off yourself and onto 'management':

DRESS CODE

- Smart, casual, clean, hygienic, no rips or tears

- No gang colors

- Upper body must be covered

- No indecent exposure, or clothing containing offensive words or pornographic images

- No sportswear, workwear, singlets, fighting clothing brands, thongs, sneakers or skate shoes

If you have the advantage of a female crowd controller or hostess at the door with you, encourage them to make the decisions on dress code as people generally find women more difficult to argue with on fashion issues.

In addition, try to refuse people entry on dress code at the start of the line so they do not feel an entitlement to enter the venue on the basis that they have been, "lining up for ages."

CANNED ROUTINE

1. You spot somebody in a group who is definitely or arguably wearing something contrary to the dress code, and do not want them in the venue.

2. You say, "Hi guys, I have a feeling that 33% of you are not going to like me tonight."

3. When they ask why, you say, "Well, two of you are really well dressed, but unfortunately we have a dress code after 6pm and do not allow skate shoes. So even though they are a great pair of shoes and I am sure they are expensive, unfortunately I have to say 'no' to your friend tonight."

4. Usually, they will ask you to make an exception, offer you money, etc. to let their friend inside the venue.

5. By now you have had more time to assess whether you want them inside the venue because, e.g. they are there with a large group of friends whose business the venue wants, they are under the intoxication limit, they are friendly, etc.

6. If you refuse them entry at this point, then do so with <u>intention</u> and to persuade them to leave the line, encourage them to go to a venue with a less strict dress code.

7. If you do decide to let them into the venue, then give them a strict warning that you do not want to see them near the entrance in, eg. the smoking area, because that will make your life difficult when refusing other patrons entry on dress code issues.

Example 1 - One night we had three fights inside a club involving a group of gang members who were all wearing singlets and shirts with no collars. To encourage the gang members already inside the premises to leave, I refused other gang members at the door based on them not wearing a collared shirt with sleeves. Eventually their friends came to the front door to see why their friends weren't getting in and I politely explained that after 10pm there is a stricter dress code (I had already built a rapport with them by making friends on earlier nights as discussed at Tip 24). Once the gang members left the venue to go somewhere where their friends could get in, I then carried on letting in non-gang members who were not wearing collars or sleeves.

Example 2 - I was walking past the line outside the club one night and was overpowered by the smell emanating from a guy in the line. He seemed to think it was funny and the other people in the line clearly did not. I had no proof that he was the source of the smell and he did not appear intoxicated enough to refuse him on that basis. Racking my mind for reasons not to let him in, I noticed his friend was wearing shoes which were arguably sneakers and decided to refuse the friend entry. The smelly AIP and his friends were therefore forced to leave the line to stay with their friend.

TIP #6

Utilize ID checks, references to Private Parties, the venue being 'female friendly', and refusal of friends to refuse Annoying Intoxicated Patrons entry, without directly stating why you want to refuse them. This avoids unnecessary confrontation and can be used subtly with pre-arranged signals with the other doormen such as asking if they want a chewing gum, etc. to signal who you want to refuse entry. Slow people down either with the line or by tying them up in conversation as they approach the entry, to give you a chance to decide whether you want them inside or not. If there is a line, or groups are hovering around outside the venue, observe them without bringing yourself to their attention, to try and gauge an idea of their state of mind. Again, try to refuse them on these grounds when they are still early in the line so they do not feel an entitlement to enter the venue by lining up for a long time.

Example 1 - I once wanted to refuse a group of sleazy looking male AIPs whom I knew from past experience were highly likely to cause trouble with girls in the venue later in the night. When one of them showed me a drivers' license from another State rather than one from the current State or a passport, I decided to seize on this and refused him entry, stating that Liquor Licensing were coming through the venue shortly and a driver's licence from the current State was needed. I then offered them some free passes to another venue (which I knew was closed at that time) to show my goodwill and they left after shaking my hand and thanking me.

Example 2 - A large bucks night arrived at the venue on a night when my security team was understaffed and I knew they would be trouble later in the night. I refused them on the ground that the venue was 'female friendly' and so did not allow in large groups of guys. To soften the blow, I then redirected them to a cheap strip club down the road which I knew would be suitable for their occasion and told them to tell the security down there that I had recommended them, to which they happily left thinking I was the nicest bouncer in the world.

TIP #7

Use the **good guy/bad guy** approach. This old, "Don't shoot the messenger" approach is invaluable in the crowd control profession and can be used in many situations to deflect the AIP's attention off yourself and onto somebody else who is more difficult to rationalize with. This can be done in lots of ways such as subtly holding your earpiece, looking at the camera and pretending to speak to the manager on your microphone, or pretending to get a signal from a bar person and nodding at them as though you are following their instruction.

Example - You do not want a large group of drunk AIPs in the venue because you sense they will be trouble later on. Get one doorman (bad guy) to refuse them entry on the ground they are too intoxicated, or find a reason such as they are wearing the wrong shoes or their jeans are ripped, etc. Then rotate that doorman away from the front door where the new doorman (good guy) can agree with the AIPs that the first doorman is a loser, too strict, etc. but yet emphasize that the first doorman is his senior so he is unable to let them in. When done with <u>intention</u> and empathy, the group will usually give up eventually or ask to see the manager, in which case you signal to the manager that you do not want them in and then go through the same approach again with the manager as the bad guy.

TIP #8

If you want to refuse a group entry because perhaps they seem aggressive or you just sense they will be trouble but cannot think of any reason to legitimately refuse them, just get them to line up or **stop the line** (this can be made to appear normal as many venues encourage crowd controllers to maintain a line outside the venue, to create the apparency that the venue is busy). If they are of an aggressive nature, the longer you leave them in the line the angrier they are going to get and hopefully will either leave or become more overtly aggressive, providing you with the perfect excuse to now not let them in.

Example - As a group approaches the club, they are shouting out at every girl they walk past in an intimidating and sleazy way. If there is no line, ask them to jump in line for a while. Look at one of them in a way that is not aggressive, but yet still authoritative. When he asks you what you are staring at say something like, "Didn't I kick you out last week?" and as he continues to deny it just keep looking at him without showing aggression. If the AIP is friendly enough then you can both just laugh it off, but if he is already in an aggressive mode, he will probably try and take you on accusing you of being arrogant, etc. Let this sizzle for just long enough to get him to abuse you and thus give you a reason to deny him entry, which will be valid in the eyes of his friends and the surrounding bystanders. It is important that the bystanders and his friends agree that the AIP is being aggressive towards you without thinking that you sparked the aggression, because otherwise the situation can very quickly deteriorate.

TIP #9

If the line is long and there are some AIPs you do not want in, approach them as if doing them a favor and let them know that the venue is at capacity and although they are free to line up, they **probably won't get in for several hours or at all that night**. If they offer you money to get in and start spitting out names of people they know in an attempt to pass the line, just say that it isn't your call. Defer the decision-making responsibility for people skipping the line onto another crowd controller or the manager, who is further away and harder for the AIPs to communicate with.

I note that this technique works beautifully if you use it on a member of the group whom you have assessed does not want to come into the venue anyway.

Example - There is a bucks night, it is now 2am and after watching the group in line for some time you notice one of the guys looking tired and trying to persuade the group to go for fast food somewhere. It is obvious that he just wants to go home without saying so, so seize this moment and advise him they probably won't get in and he can take it from there in persuading the group out of the line.

TIP #10

Stare people down before they enter the venue. If you see potential trouble makers approaching the venue, hold a fixed stare at them in an authoritative yet not aggressive manner. Often they will start straightening up when you do this and you can then give them a warning which is serious yet kept fun with a twinkle in your eye such as, "Oh great, more (Irish, Brits, American, whatever) people! It seems all the trouble I have had tonight has been caused by the damn...! Now you're not going to cause any trouble are you boys, you wouldn't go out of your way to create grief for me, would you?" They will usually laugh because they like being branded as trouble makers, yet you would have got them on side before they enter. This can be played on later in the night if they cause trouble by referring to your earlier warning before they came in.

As you are staring people down, you can also fabricate a connection to them by asking where they are from and pretending to know somebody they know, or have gone to a place they lived in, etc. to play off later.

TIP #11

Stay in communication with the manager. Often confrontations start up because of arbitrary rules that do not make sense to people. Sometimes arbitrary rules are necessary such as, 'no drinks outside the front of the venue', 'no smoking', etc. and so you can deal with these without the need to contact the manager. However, on other occasions the rule may not need to be applied either on that night or in general and has come into being as a result of a miscommunication or without taking into account the present facts. When in doubt, always clarify the rules with the manager or head of security, to get it straight from the horse's mouth and question the rules if you cannot understand why they are being applied.

Example - The normal dress code for the club does not allow sneakers. You start refusing people on a Wednesday night for wearing sneakers and they become agitated because it is a quiet night inside the club and they cannot understand why sneakers are not allowed. You contact the manager to help deal with the situation and find that the rule forbidding sneakers only applies on Friday and Saturday nights and not Wednesdays.

TIP #12

Remain vigilant at all times. As a crowd controller you should always be watching into the distance to anticipate situations and this is particularly important on the front door. If violence appears imminent it is that few seconds you gained from detecting the situation early that will make all the difference. As a professional crowd controller you must remain alert and not distracted by girls, your new smartphone or anything else. Bouncing is a fun job so you should have fun joking around with people, etc. but put effort into developing that sixth spider sense that keeps you constantly aware of everything which is going on around you.

TIP #13

Take out AIP insurance. If you let in somebody you don't really want in, if appropriate you can ask to hold onto their driver's licence as insurance, to make sure they behave themselves so they can get it back. Do not accept a useless card such as a discount card they try to palm off to you as they will not care if they get it back, which is counterproductive. However, don't take this too far! When they ask for their ID back despite misbehaving, you do not want to be perceived as stealing the licence, which can be a grey area with police.

TIP #14

Maintain an appearance of consistency with rules. Although you will constantly be bending the rules for people who know management, are regulars, are gang affiliated, etc. you must maintain at least an appearance of being consistent in the application of the rules to everyone to avoid them feeling discriminated against. Therefore, where necessary, at least pretend to check their stamp, etc. if you are giving them priority entry, to create the appearance that they have already been inside the venue, so the crowd who may have been lining up for ages does not become aggravated by you.

TIP #15

Carry a lighter, cigarettes and chewing gum. Many times when people get kicked out and hang around at the door threatening me, I get them talking by asking what is going on? Then, as they start to calm down a bit from talking about the problem, I offer them a cigarette or some chewing gum while they are waiting for a taxi, or their friends. This creates an instant rapport with them.

When people go out the front of the venue to smoke you can also use this opportunity to make friends and show what a nice guy you are by lighting up their cigarette. Having a group of allied smokers out the front of the venue can be invaluable when there are evictions and you need some backup from patrons to calm AIPs down and stop them getting back in the venue.

TIP #16

Make friends with crowd controllers from other venues, off duty police officers and generally huge guys and let them skip the line, as they will be invaluable if trouble starts later on. It is also useful to have the phone numbers of head doormen from other venues so you can stay in touch and warn each other about trouble makers around the area, where the police are and provide each other with backup when urgently required.

TIP #17

Check older womens' IDs. Virtually every night there is an awkward moment when out of a group of older women you only check the ID of the one who looks the youngest. After many experiences of unintentionally offending older women, I have learned that it is easier to just ask the whole group for ID and 9 times out of 10 they will absolutely love you for it and you will have made their year!! Now and again they will protest, arguing they are obviously over the age limit in which case you just say it is company policy to check every ID.

If you do not feel comfortable asking a clearly older woman for her ID and she asks why you didn't check it, just dodge the bullet by saying it's because you thought she was a VIP or the name of some movie star.

TIP #18

If somebody is hanging around on the door in a friendly but yet annoying manner, which happens virtually every night in the club world, you can get rid of them by **using flattery to redirect their attention** and encourage them to move on subtly without causing offense.

Example - When an AIP is excessively talking to you on the door because perhaps they have attended the venue alone or all their friends have left and they are beginning to test your patience, say something like the following to redirect their attention and move them off: "Dude you could have your pick of any girl in here.

You should get in there and put a smile on their faces," and then with <u>*intention*</u> *direct them back into or out of the venue.*

TIP #19

Be cautious of taking tips. You should be able to judge whether a tip is obligation free or not, but be cautious as often an innocent favor of getting someone through the line for example can result in all sorts of problems when the AIP continuously comes back to you for favors, putting you in an awkward position in front of management and your security team.

TIP #20

Know all the streets and landmarks around you in case you need to call the police or ambulance quickly. Also, get to know the details of other venues nearby so if you want to refuse somebody entry, you can tactfully suggest other venues to them which have a more relaxed dress code and expectations of their clientele. The same goes for taxi ranks when you want to encourage somebody to head home for the night.

TIP #21

Keep the local police and your security company's phone numbers on **speed dial** in case you need urgent backup.

TIP #22

If refusing entry to somebody after closing time and they are, for example, busting for the toilet, ensure you **know where the nearest toilet is** to soften the blow of refusing them entry, if you know management does not want them in.

TIP #23

Invest in decent equipment such as your own earpiece for hygiene purposes, comfortable shoes, and thermal gear if you are outside all night. A detachable ID card lanyard and detachable tie is also important, so these items cannot be used to strangle you during a confrontation. A small torch is also very useful for checking handbags and IDs and doubles as a legitimate item that can be carried for protection with the hard bottom of the torch, if absolutely necessary, without you being accused of concealing a weapon.

TIP #24

Make friends with underworld types. Even though I may not approve of the nature of some of their work, I know when I am out-gunned and have found it consistently easier to get along with these guys for the purpose of being an effective crowd controller, than trying to go Rambo on them and ending up in the morgue. I have also found it far easier to keep gang members in line by approaching their leader whom I have already befriended and asking them to keep their guys in line. This is far better than trying to take on some young punk with an axe to grind. Nine times out of ten this works because the leaders usually just want to keep a low profile and these types of antics are bad for their business and reputation.

When these guys come to the venue, shake their hands and let them skip the line and your life and the survival of the venue will be far better off because of it. To maintain some leverage over them, I usually still get some or all of them to jump in the VIP line rather than entering the venue straight away so I can still go through the process of checking their IDs and having a chat before they enter to get them onside and show them that I still have a job to do.

It is also worth noting that many venues do have underworld affiliations which you should become aware of so you know the preferred gang(s) for that venue and therefore have advance warning if you sense trouble will begin. If you have trouble with gangs, let the manager know rather than trying to deal with it yourself so they can use their connections or the police to resolve the issue.

If you have to handle the situation yourself, try to make it appear you are on the gang's side by telling the one you have the best relationship with that you just heard the police are on their way to do a sting, or telling them the inside scoop on some other venue that is open that night to encourage them to go check it out.

2 SNEAKING IN

TIP #25

When checking IDs on the front door, **keep a list of zodiac signs** (star signs) on your phone, in your notebook, etc. to test suspected underagers' signs match up with their ID. If you have learned which zodiac sign corresponds with each month of dates, you can also use this as a test by making a comment relevant to their zodiac sign and judging whether they know what you are talking about. E.g. if they are a Leo, you can say, "You're not planning on growling at the girls tonight are you?" or if they are a Virgo you can play around by asking if they plan on losing their virginity tonight, if they appear the kind of person who will laugh along with that joke and not take you seriously. If they don't get the joke, then ask what zodiac sign they are and if it is not the sign on the ID, do not let them in. They may respond by saying they do not believe in zodiac signs but just about everybody knows their zodiac sign even if they do not believe in them, so don't let them fool you.

I also note that even if you do not know which star sign is which, just asking this question anyway is a great intoxication test as you can use it to assess how long it takes for them to answer the question, regardless of whether their response was correct or not.

TIP #26

Know the law concerning whether or not you can confiscate fake IDs as it varies from State to State and, if in doubt, don't bother confiscating the fake ID but rather just don't let the person in. Most States have a law that personally fines crowd controllers, venue managers and venues for having underagers in the venue, so when underagers or friends persist in trying to convince you to let them in, make sure they understand that you will be personally fined if you let them in, so they can see it is not just some faceless venue which gets the fine.

TIP #27

Be particularly watchful of expired IDs as sometimes these have been given to somebody who looks like the person in the ID because the original holder no longer needs it.

TIP #28

If you suspect someone is using a fake ID, say with intention and shock that **you know the person in the ID** and watch their response. If it is fake, they will often admit it and ask to be let in anyway because you now have a common friend.

TIP #29

Carry a notebook to test that **peoples' signatures** match up with their ID.

TIP #30

Keep an eye on the **area surrounding the venue** as underagers may be hovering around awkwardly while waiting for a friend to imprint their stamp on to the other's arm, or pass on their ID which can give you clues as to who to be stricter on.

TIP #31

Keep a close eye on who is in the **smokers' area** outside the front of the venue as sometimes people with no ID will casually blend in with the smokers, so they can merge in the venue with the other smokers as though they had already been inside. Equally, keep an eye on anybody leaving the venue to meet people as the person they are meeting may try to blend in as though they have already been inside.

TIP #32

Be cautious of people who are **overly friendly** to you prior to going in, by stating that, e.g. they are waiting for somebody outside and then striking up a conversation with you in the hope that you forget to ask them for ID.

Example - I was once slapped with a $400 fine for letting in a very attractive girl who engaged me in a conversation about other crowd controllers she knew, etc. and after around 15 minutes I shamefully completely forgot to check her ID. The police saw that I had let her in and gave me an on the spot fine because they knew her to be a prostitute who was 13 years old!!! I would have picked her as at least 22 years old and ordinarily still would have checked her ID to be safe. Needless to say, I have never repeated the mistake of becoming overly comfortable with people on the front door!

TIP #33

As you are checking IDs, watch peoples' friends **trying to distract you** with handshakes, asking if the manager is in, whether it is busy inside, etc. as they will use this to distract you from assessing the ID properly.

TIP #34

Encourage people to be **stamped** as they leave the venue, so it is easier for you to see if they have already been inside. If management does not have this policy, encourage them to institute it.

TIP #35

Watch for the following **signs of lying**: the suspected underager excessively talks and looks flushed or out of breath, they get jumpy when you stare at them for a few seconds and start impatiently protesting how old they are and come up with overly detailed stories about why they do not have ID. A lot has been written on how to detect lying, so I would encourage you to study this subject in more detail as it is a great skill to have on the door.

TIP #36

If someone begs you to enter the venue to go to the toilet or just to give somebody their car keys, ATM card, etc. then ask them to **leave something personal with you** such as their own keys, to increase the chance that they come back to you and don't disappear into the crowd without showing their ID.

3 COPPING ABUSE

TIP #37

Communicate with and listen to people. When an Annoying Intoxicated Patron starts beating their chest and amplifying anger at you they are often just using this as a tool to get your attention so they will be listened to. You would be surprised how much you can cool them down by genuinely paying them attention and using empathy to acknowledge them with phrases such as, "Oh, ok," "Now I understand," "I really do get that," "I got it," and so on. Listening to people does not mean you have to follow what they are asking you to do, but rather it can be utilized as a tool to drain their anger so they become more rational and easier to deal with. Remember, **Communication is King!**

In addition, try to avoid accusative phrases such as, "You are drunk," "You are wrong," "You started the fight," and so on. Instead, soften your wording with phrases like, "It has been brought to my attention that you were drinking from a hip flask inside the venue," "According to the manager you were behind the bar area trying to grab the vodka bottle," "I believe you are too intoxicated tonight," etc. Phrases like this make it harder for the AIP to argue with you because you are stating an opinion, rather than a fact, and everybody is entitled to an opinion.

TIP #38

Whenever I get abused on the door I use a technique made famous by the world renowned pickup artist, Mystery, called '**ghosting**'. Basically ghosting involves just allowing the abuse to pass straight through you as if you were a ghost and maintaining your enthusiasm for what you are doing. It is amazing how effective this can be and people eventually give up when they realize they are having no effect on you.

AIPs will constantly attempt to introvert you throughout the night by turning your attention onto yourself instead of having it on them or somewhere else away from yourself. When they try to introvert you, just ghost it and let it pass straight through you.

Example 1 - AIP says, "Look at this idiot, do you even know how to spell 'intoxicated'?" You simply allow this to go straight through without letting it offend you and respond with something witty such as, "It is very interesting that the world's smartest man, Chris Langan, is a nightclub bouncer." When they say, "So what are you saying, you're the world's smartest man?", you can just smile, ghost their comment and respond with, "Very interesting...good stuff!" and don't play into their trap.

Example 2 - AIP says, "Look at this skinny dude. Are you even a bouncer or the door bitch?" Don't allow them to introvert you by making you think you are too underweight for your job, etc. and instead just ghost it and respond with something witty like, "Nah dude, I am just the door bitch and its going to take a lot more to get in my pants than a smart ass comment like that...You could at least buy me dinner first!" They will usually laugh at this point as they realize their antagonism is having no affect on you.

TIP #39

If you find there are certain areas that you are touchy on and ghosting does not work for you on that particular area then **get a friend to practice insulting you** on those areas. Just like in martial arts training, the more you do it over and over again the more control you will gain over it and the less it will affect you. Every time you get abused from now on see it as a little game of yours to test whether you can successfully ghost it and if not, then note this area as a weakness for you to practice with a friend.

TIP #40

When faced with an oppositional statement such as, "What are you going to do about it?", don't play their game by reacting aggressively. **Just ghost it, side step the question** and with <u>intention</u> say a response such as, "I am going to very politely request that you no longer do X" or "Nothing at all, but our lovely manager over there would be very upset if you continued to do X, so we'd really appreciate if you could no longer do it." Usually the AIP will feel foolish if they continue to push forward aggressively once you have already smoothly side stepped them and they will start listening more to you to save face to their group.

TIP #41

People will often not respond well to you merely because you are an authority figure and not because of anything you personally have done. It is therefore vital to **relate to people**, so they can actually communicate with you and aren't busy talking to you as if you were some authority figure in their past, with whom they may have had a bad experience.

One of the best ways to relate to people is to **mirror their demeanor**. If a guy is hunched over and talking in a rough fashion, then you could mirror his mannerisms and talk in a similar way to make you more real to him, so you are therefore easier for him to communicate with. This, of course needs to be done naturally and not appear to be in any way condescending towards them.

Example 1 - A young raver guy keeps taking his shirt off in the club and sweating all over the girls next to him. You say "Duuuuddddee, having fun? Awesome man rock on! Just have to ask you to put your shirt back on as you're sweating up the place. [He laughs and puts back on shirt]. Good stuff buddy, have fun!"

Example 2 - Dignified 50 year old accountant leaves the premises carrying an open bottle of expensive champagne. You straighten up and say, "Excuse me, sir, I am terribly sorry, but you actually can't take an open bottle of champagne outside the premises. [He responds saying he isn't going to throw it out but needs to leave to pick up his son from school now]. You say, "I totally understand that, sir, how about you come back inside with me for a moment and we can get a lid for you so the champagne doesn't go flat?" As you have approached him in a polite and dignified way, he will be far more open to receiving your communication and thereby willing to work with you to resolve the problem.

TIP #42

You can also **agree with people** to help them relate to you. When AIPs become confrontational with you, the situation can very quickly deteriorate if you disagree with them on whatever their argument is, because then they become more determined to win on that particular point and it becomes harder and harder to get back to the original issue.

Example 1 - You need to get an AIP to stop dancing in a part of the bar that is reserved for eating and they laugh in your face. You could just laugh and agree with them that it is a strange rule to build reality with them, but then say words to the effect that, unfortunately, you need to enforce this rule. If you didn't build up their initial reality on you by agreeing with them and just skipped to telling them it is against the rules, they will probably not be as open to receiving your communication, because you simply are not somebody they can relate to.

Example 2 - You approach a guy looking intoxicated and ask him to leave the premises. He argues that he is not intoxicated and is just having fun after finishing his university exams. You agree with him that he should be partying and going hard after finishing exams but then defer responsibility for the decision by saying that you have caught word that Liquor Licensing is coming through shortly and so even though he is just having fun, the venue just can't risk being fined. Then suggest another venue he can go to and move him out with urgency and <u>intention</u>, to maintain credibility that Liquor Licensing is coming through shortly.

Example 3 - A guy tries to belittle you and tells you he could beat the hell out of you. Just agree with him and say that of course he could beat the hell out of you, but you are hoping it doesn't come to that. This response will be so unexpected by your aggressor, that they initially won't know how to respond, but because you have complimented and agreed with them, they won't be able to help liking you more and you can continue to smooth out the situation from there.

TIP #43

People do not like to lose and if you want to get an AIP's agreement to do something it is important that they feel they are winning, to satisfy their ego and help them save face in front of co-workers, girls and friends.

This **win/win** tactic essentially involves you taking a hard line with somebody and then relaxing it slightly, so both you and the AIP feel you have come out on top.

Example - A man is drinking alcohol outside the front of the club having a cigarette. You approach him and advise that he will need to take the drink back inside as it is outside the licensed area (hard line). He responds by saying, he will go back inside once his cigarette is finished. You agree with him that it is annoying [to build rapport] and then offer to look after his drink by placing it on the cashier's desk inside where you can see it while he finishes his cigarette (relax the hard line). He will usually agree to this and you have gotten the drink back inside (win/win).

TIP #44

To reduce your own fear, look your aggressor in the eyes. Fear is caused by the unknown, so when you look your aggressor in the eyes, not only are you showing them that you are not intimidated by them but they will become more known to you and so reduce your fear. You can also judge a lot about how somebody is going to act by their eyes.

TIP #45

NEVER EVER accept a challenge to fight anyone as you will immediately lose all bargaining power as an authority figure. If you are unable to ghost the challenge and not let it affect you, then rotate with another crowd controller to a different position to get away from the person or take a short break. You may also like to try Dalton's technique in Road House where he accepted the challenge to fight on the condition that it was outside the venue. Then when they both walked outside, Dalton walked back inside the venue and the aggressor was stopped by the front door guys. Good for a giggle anyway.

TIP #46

As Dalton says, **"Be nice until it's time not to be nice"**. Violence should be an absolute last resort. Although I have spent the majority of the last decade handling situations with the techniques in this text, there is no doubt that there have been times when you simply cannot rationalize with the aggressor and being partnered with a 7-foot former Russian police officer has certainly had its benefits. Learning a martial art to handle these situations can be life saving in those rare cases where new school techniques fail.

TIP #47

Do not feed the AIP by giving them a justification to become aggressive with you. When people look at you in a venue, often they do not even see you as a person and might be seeing you through the lens of all the other arrogant bouncers they have encountered in the past. When they are fuelled with alcohol, they may, for whatever reason, want to fight you and are waiting for you to provoke them in some way, so they can justify harming you to themselves, their friends and the police. Recognize this, keep a cool head and don't ever give someone an excuse to hit you.

Example - You evict an AIP from a venue and they hang around taunting you by saying you think are, "the king," etc. They keep on staring at you, trying to get you to stare back to justify punching you, both to themselves and also to bystanders and video cameras on the basis that you provoked them. Try to avoid eye contact with them and just act like they are not there. Don't do this in a fearful way, but just hold your ground and don't fuel their anger.

TIP #48

When you arrive to a job, treat it like a dojo where you **leave your troubles at the door** and stay in present time. If you snap at somebody because you are already angry, this can very quickly escalate because even though you might blame the world for your anger, the fact is you chose to act in that way and you must keep that urge under control.

TIP #49

When things start getting heated **just laugh and joke around** with the AIP. I have witnessed a friend of mine, Big Willie, doing this on countless occasions and the situation just immediately cooled down as if by magic. Try it!

Example - One night Willie was punched by an AIP and much to the surprise of everybody watching he just started laughing and patted the AIP on the back congratulating him on getting in a good punch. When I later asked why he responded in this way, he said simply that he had already been punched once that night and did not want to be hit again.

TIP #50

Avoid shaking AIPs' hands. I once evicted a very large and intimidating guy whom I thought was leaving without causing any trouble. Once outside he shook my hand and absolutely crushed it leaving me feeling ridiculous for having gotten into that position. To avoid the social awkwardness of not shaking hands, try doing the light fists punching on each other style of handshake or slap their hand in a friendly manner, to avoid actually shaking hands. You could also pretend to cough into your hand just before they extend theirs, so they will understand why you are not shaking it.

If you cannot avoid shaking an AIP's hand, then extend your index finger into the palm of their hand to realign your knuckles, making it much more difficult to crush yours.

TIP #51

Deter AIPs by making them feel shameful for their actions. When using this technique you must be discreet as, if you embarrass an AIP in front of others, particularly in front of the opposite sex, they will lash out at you to protect their primitive ego and it won't be pretty.

Example - After closing time one night I was asked by a lady if she could go to the bathroom. The bar had already closed 20 minutes ago and I knew that if I let her in I would have to let in the half a dozen other people who had just asked me to use the bathroom. I politely refused her entry and suddenly she unzipped her fly and threatened to urinate all over the floor of the court yard. Suddenly I had ten or so people abusing me for not letting her in and I had to think fast, because the manager had strictly said not to let anybody else in. I calmly told her that I had had enough urination for one night and she curiously asked me what I was referring to. I told her that a gentleman had urinated in the corner of the bar that night (I made it up but it seemed to work) and how disgusted I was by him. She agreed and said that that was absolutely foul. I agreed with her and suggested that perhaps it would be best to zip her fly back up and pretend this never happened, to which she agreed and quietly wandered off.

TIP #52

Utilize AIPs' friends against them. Often when an AIP is being rowdy you can use their friends to keep them in line with methods such as:

a) Making friends with their friends either by joking around with them when they go outside for a cigarette, complimenting them on their dance moves, taking a photo of the group for them early in the night, and so on. Then, as you give a warning to the AIP, appoint their friend your **deputy babysitter** by shaking the friend's hand and asking them to keep the AIP in line; and

b) Threatening to evict their entire group, to use **peer pressure** against them (but keep their group on side, by saying, e.g. "However, I don't want that anymore than you do as I am sure you are all having fun!"). This will often be enough to encourage an AIP's friends to keep them in line. I note that this tactic works particularly well when the group has just bought a round of drinks, or one of their friends has just met a girl and started dancing, etc.

TIP #53

Point out cameras. Unless they have drunk obscene amounts of alcohol or are on drugs, an AIP will usually be far less willing to act in a violent or unruly manner if they know there will be evidence left of them doing so. I often point out the cameras in a way which appears to be helping them such as, "I understand dude, but that's probably not the best idea since there are cameras up there which the coppers will get hold of and use against you, even though you were just looking after your buddy."

TIP #54

Do not give AIPs your full name or personal details such as your football club, etc. as they could use this to gain leverage over you by taunting you with the threat of something occurring to you outside of work. In this day and age of Google, various social networking sites and mobile smart phones, it has become extremely easy to perform quick internet background checks on people. If you would like to see what is on the internet about you, I would recommend signing up for a subscription at www.spokeo.com, which performs a very broad search of virtually all social networking sites and a deep search engine search so you are forewarned about what people can find out about you.

TIP #55

Know your limits.

Example 1 - I once had a group of guys arrive outside of the bar I was working at and started smashing up the cars out the front with baseball bats. A staff member came running outside and asked me to get the guys off the cars as they were staff members' cars. I knew that these guys meant business and the threat level was very high so instead I focused my attention on minimizing the damage by getting everyone who was outside to come inside the venue and sit tight while the police were called.

Example 2 - Another night I had a very aggressive gang demanding entrance to the club and claiming to know the manager. The manager had told me earlier that they were coming down and not to let them inside under any circumstances. As one of the gang members pointed to his pocket to indicate a weapon, I bought time by pretending to misunderstand their having said they knew the manager. I then called the police immediately while pretending to look for the manager and told the gang that the manager would be down in a moment while I sat tight waiting for the police.

TIP #56

Don't be a hero. I have had many experiences in venues where something happens off site, such as vandalism or an assault, and the crowd has turned against me for not getting involved. Once you step off the venue, know that you are no longer protected by video cameras, backup from other crowd controllers, insurance coverage and so on, because you are now acting outside the scope of your employment. You are not paid to get involved in matters off the venue's premises so don't do so unless absolutely necessary.

TIP #57

Do not let your guard down when walking to your car at the end of the night, particularly if you were involved in antagonistic instances earlier. Try and walk in numbers if possible, or park somewhere well lit and with other people around, as a deterrent to AIPs following you at the end of the night.

Example - I once had a car follow me after I left work and the driver pointed a gun at me insisting I get in the car. To this day I do not know exactly what his motive was, but I managed to deter him by running back near the club where I knew there were security cameras and other people, and it was those environmental factors which saved me on that occasion.

4 ROAMING THE JUNGLE

TIP #58

When inside the venue, you will either be at a fixed static position, or roaming around. While inside, you should constantly be scanning the crowd and proactively taking steps to **prevent incidents before they occur**. If there are no service staff at your venue who pick up empty glasses, then do this yourself, particularly around trouble spots such as the front door, so they cannot be used as weapons later on and also as an excuse to move within groups of potentially troublesome people, so you can be in a closer position to gauge their behavior. You should also be actively on the lookout for hazards such as spilt drinks and glasses on the floor, so you can alert the service staff to attend to it and thus reduce the risk of accidents happening.

TIP #59

Learn the names of different sections in the venue and the other security and staff's names. Communication is everything in security and there is nothing worse than some idiot on the radio calling you to a location at 'the bar' when there are five different bars in the venue! You should also conduct radio checks every few hours and, especially if you have not heard anything on the radio for a while and check your earpiece has not become clogged up, which the clear tube earpieces in particular often do.

Become familiar with the **hand signals** your security team uses. The signals vary from venue to venue, but a rough guide of common signals include:

1. Get attention - waive one open hand;

2. Signal person for removal - put one closed fist in the air;

3. Signal for another crowd controller to come to you - place one hand on your head;

4. Fight - Cross your hands over your head and waive each hand to the left and right; and

5. All good - Place both thumbs up in the air.

TIP #60

Do not abandon your position until your team is aware you are doing so. If you are on the front door, in particular, this is absolutely vital as AIPs can just walk in and you are then left having to get them out, which is a lot harder than stopping them at the door. If you are inside the venue, you are the eyes and ears of the head doorman so if you just walk off to the toilet for fifteen minutes, anything could happen inside and the head doorman will not know until it is too late.

TIP #61

Watch for the following signs of intoxication: The Annoying Intoxicated Patron speaks in a slow and focused way; they are loud and chatty with their friends but as you approach they give 'yes' and 'no' answers, to avoid giving away their intoxication by the way they talk; they won't look you in the eye or, instead really stare at you; they are overly flirtatious with the opposite sex; buy strangers drinks; stare into space or at the cash machine for unnecessarily long; are held up by a friend while standing or are spending overly long periods in the bathroom. If you think somebody is too intoxicated and they have not yet entered the venue, slow them down and chat with them for a while, asking if they have been to any other good venues that night, what the occasion for them coming out is, etc. to get them to talk more to see if they are drunk.

TIP #62

If you detect somebody is getting too intoxicated, then **move in early and offer them some water**. This can be done very casually to avoid embarrassing them by just stating that it is getting hot inside and suggesting in an authoritative way that they have some water to avoid overheating. Either this in itself will prevent the person getting so intoxicated that they need to be evicted or it will at least position you as the good guy in the event you need to evict them later on.

TIP #63

Watch your body language. As an authority figure, you must always appear emotionally balanced or you will lose your bargaining power.

a) Too many times I have seen bouncers clenching their fists when they get angry, which immediately provokes AIPs to defend themselves and suddenly the fireworks begin. When dealing with people always **keep your hands out in front** in an open fashion. This stance does not look threatening, yet allows you to react quickly if you are attacked. Sometimes when I am evicting female AIPs and they are refusing to leave I will keep my hands up and lightly nudge them along with my elbows, so I am still applying force but it looks better to the crowd because my hands are up.

b) **Avoid crossing your arms when talking to AIPs** as this will indicate that you are not listening to them (even if you are) causing them to become more and more dramatic to get their point across. That being said, when it gets to a point where they are just not getting the message and hassling you continuously, it can be effective to cross your arms and ignore them completely, so they will eventually realize they are having no effect on you and leave; and

c) Maintain **good eye contact** when talking to people to show you are listening to and respect them.

TIP #64

There is an old saying that, "**Appearance is Everything**." You may be the most well intentioned person in the world but this amounts to nothing if you are not showing it. In addition to your body language, always make sure your appearance is suitable of an authority figure in your position. If your shirt is hanging out, your hair is messy, and you are playing on your phone in front of people all night, who on earth is going to take you seriously?? To increase your bargaining power make sure you look the part.

You may resent this comment as something your mother would tell you but think about this for a moment, whose directions are you more likely to respect: a teacher-like gentlemen wearing a tie and with combed hair or a miserable looking dude wearing a torn Jim Beam t-shirt and thongs with an unshaven scruffy looking face?

TIP #65

Use a mixture of warnings and the good guy/bad guy approach. When roaming around inside the venue, you should be constantly hanging around AIPs, letting them know you are watching them so they do not get too out of control and providing them with numerous warnings to make the eviction process easier if it is to occur later on, as discussed in more detail in the following Chapter at Tip 71. Merging these warnings with the good guy/bad guy approach also helps to deflect the attention off yourself as the decision maker.

Example 1 - If a group of AIPs are getting rowdy and bumping into people, etc. you could say, "Hey guys, I understand you are all buddies and I get that you are just having fun, but if you bump into someone else then it becomes my job to do something about it, so I need you to settle down a little. I am sure you guys don't want to leave and I sure as hell don't want to ruin your night because you look like cool guys, so let's just take easy, eh?"

Example 2 - If a group of guys are doing shots and doubling up on their drinks, then be proactive and approach them with a standard line such as, "Hi guys, I see you are doing heaps of shots, which is cool and I realize you are just having fun but the issue is that the cops come in here all the time and if they see that, then we could be fined a lot of money because technically you are showing signs of intoxication, which can mean pretty much whatever the cops want it to mean (put the cops in as the bad guys and you the good guy). How about just pacing the drinks, having water between them and not carrying around two drinks for yourself, as that is exactly what the cops look for when they fine us. Apart from that, enjoy yourselves and have a good night."

Example 3 - "Excuse me, sir, I know it's annoying (gain rapport by showing understanding) but unfortunately the manager has requested that you remove your hat inside (deflects attention on to the manager)." Then when the AIP argues that it is ridiculous, they spend thousands of dollars a week at the venue, etc. you can simply nod in agreement but without giving in and they will often give up shortly afterwards because you are not the decision maker, the 'manager' is (the bad guy).

TIP #66

Maintain a good relationship with service staff. They are your eyes and ears inside the venue and often in the best position to determine who you need to keep an eye on or evict.

TIP #67

Watch that service staff do not take other peoples' drinks and when people go outside or to an area of the venue you cannot take drinks into, make sure they place the drinks somewhere safe, such as on a small table inside at the cashier's desk. Nothing creates an argument faster than a drunk having their precious drink taken from them!

TIP #68

Maintain a close watch on drunk girls. It sounds obvious but drunk girls seem to be the cause of 99% of fights by either being too flirtatious, losing their purses and then accusing people of taking them or by drunk guys staking the girl as theirs for the night and other guys competing for her while she isn't being forceful enough in refusing them. A charming bastard like you would probably be watching the girls anyway but just keep a little extra eye out.

TIP #69

Make friends with the regulars of the venue. They have an interest in keeping the venue safe and will often act as your eyes and ears. I like to think of them as my unofficial deputies and when things get out of control they will often help you to cool the situation.

TIP #70

Ally yourself with those in high social standing, so that AIPs realize that by causing you grief it will affect other areas of their life.

Example - A group of AIPs are shouting in the club and acting inappropriately. Earlier in the night you complimented one of the beautiful girls in their group by joking around calling her Xena Warrior Princess or something when she didn't smile as you checked her ID, which made her laugh. As you approach the group of guys she is with, have another joke with her and make it clear to the guys that you have her on side (without appearing to be flirting with her which could aggravate the situation). As they start trying to toy around with you, the girl will then usually cool them down and ask you if everything's cool, etc. to handle the situation.

5 EVICTIONS

Every eviction is different and different tactics work better for different people. However, as themed throughout the following Tips, the key to a successful eviction is applying the correct gradient to the situation to allow yourself room to move. Although evictions will test your patience and it can be far more tempting to just run in and drag them out by their neck, unfortunately this approach has too many implications for you and the venue (not to mention the amount of boring reports you have to write at the end of the night, usually on your own time) so needs to be avoided until absolutely necessary.

TIP #71

Use warnings to increase your bargaining power.

When you want to evict an unruly patron, give them an initial warning(s) to soften the blow of the final eviction.

CANNED ROUTINE 1

1. "Excuse me, sir! I realize you're just having fun, but your constant swearing out loud is not appropriate for this venue and I would appreciate it if you could keep it down a bit."

Then when they predictably continue swearing loudly, you can come up a second time looking slightly sterner and give a stronger warning.

2. "Sorry, sir, I asked you to stop swearing earlier. If this continues you will need to leave the premises."

AIPs ordinarily like to roam free and so may resent your attempt to control them and although agreeing to your face, will continue to swear after you have gone. Simply watch them from a distance and when the swearing continues, return with backup and say:

3. "Ok, buddy, I gave you several warnings but as you have continued to swear loudly I now have to ask you to leave!"

The AIP will initially tell you to get lost, at which point you can use other tactics to gain bargaining power such as the win/win tactic discussed in more detail in the following Tip, whereby after initially refusing to leave they ask, "Can I at least finish my drink?" to which you agree, and thereby increase your bargaining power by getting their agreement to leave.

CANNED ROUTINE 2

The following is an example of the use of warnings at the cross over time in the night when the dress code becomes stricter.

"6:30pm: Excuse me guys, unfortunately after 7pm our dress code doesn't allow sandals, so you will need to either leave or change to shoes by that time." People will generally nod in agreement when you say this.

Occasionally somebody will challenge it, in which case you lessen the blow by saying, e.g. "Sorry about that sir, you are of course welcome to finish your drink before you leave. For future reference, Saturday night is our busiest night so we have a tighter dress code."

6:45pm: "Hi guys, just a quick reminder that you have around 15 minutes to finish up before the dress code becomes stricter."

7:00pm: "Hi guys, just need to finish up now and head toward the exit door, please." Then just stand there awkwardly looking at them without saying anything, and they will usually start standing up and finishing drinks, at which point you make small talk such as, "I hope you had a nice night" and so on and gradually move away once they start walking towards the exit, so they don't feel that you are 'evicting' them.

TIP #72

If warnings fail to bring the AIP under control, then steepen the gradient by trying the **win/win** tactic outlined at Tip 43 which involves taking a hard line and then relaxing it so they feel they are gaining something.

Example - You have advised an AIP after several warnings that they are too intoxicated and need to leave the premises (hard line). They ridicule you, laugh amongst themselves and continue drinking their drink. You say, "Come on buddy, time to go" and place your hand on his arm. Once he feels out-gunned he may ask if he could at least finish his drink. At this point you agree (relax the hard line) and babysit him for the next few minutes prior to the eviction while he finishes his drink (win/win).

TIP #73

If an incident has suddenly occurred such as the manager approached you and asked you to remove somebody, so there is little room for warnings and other lower gradient approaches, you can very rapidly increase your bargaining power over the AIP by asking them with intention to **come outside for a discussion** so you can *hear them better and find out what is going on* (or use one of the other tricks mentioned at TIP #86). You then gain substantial power over them as they are away from their friends, often have a drink still inside, need to tell their friends they are leaving, need to go to the toilet before they leave, etc.

You can then transition into several tactics depending on the circumstances:

Option 1- If they become rude and aggressive, do not let them back inside.

Option 2- If they demand to see the manager, you call the manager outside who will assess the situation and if they do not let them back inside, you can merge into the good guy/bad guy routine with the manager as the bad guy.

Option 3- The AIP agrees to leave after they have spoken to their friends, finished their drink, grabbed their jacket, and so on. You gain leverage over them by asking to hold on to their driver's licence or getting a wholehearted promise that they will come back outside along with their agreement to go inside with another crowd controller to babysit them. You then ensure they leave.

TIP #74

When commencing an eviction, be extremely cautious of your **body language** as you do not want to appear to be a physical threat to the person until it is absolutely necessary. Evictions should therefore be commenced by approaching the person on a 45 degree angle and touching them on the elbow to attract their attention before talking to them. When you touch them, you should keep your hand in that position while talking to them and guiding with your other hand to where you want them to go. By having one hand in physical contact with the AIP's elbow, you can also use that elbow to move them away from you or transition into a wrist lock if they suddenly lash out at you.

TIP #75

When beginning an eviction **always send in the crowd controller with the best verbal ability first**. An articulate crowd controller can often charm their way through an eviction and appear terribly diplomatic throughout the whole process saving a lot of unnecessary trouble. Often they will use phrases like, "Time to call it a night guys," "Looks like you've had a little too much fun tonight, but there's always next weekend," "Allow me to call a taxi for you madam," etc. to make the eviction seem less personal and allow the AIP to retain their dignity. If, however, their good guy approach fails, they can always suggest to the AIP that the larger, meaner looking 'bouncer' in the background will have to step in, allowing room to move in their negotiation to get the patron out.

Example - A few times at work I was partnered up with a virtually useless bouncer who was grossly overweight, had a look of absolute misery on his face and refused to ever talk to anyone or take off his sunglasses. In truth the guy was an absolute teddy bear who wouldn't hurt a fly but on several occasions all I had to do was point at him and tell the group I didn't want to have to get the big guy in the sunglasses and that was enough to subdue the group.

TIP #76

Instead of walking the person out yourself, which can be embarrassing for the AIP, **give their friends the opportunity to walk their friend out first.** This way you transfer responsibility for the eviction to their friends who will often thank you for your courtesy and comply, so they have control of the eviction and reduce the risk of their friend getting hurt. If the friends are slow to walk the person out of the venue, you can just hang back for a few minutes within their view and watch, to let them know you have not forgotten and usually they will eventually go.

This tactic works particularly well with friends of staff-members as the friends often think they have a free pass to drink as much as they want. You can then encourage the staff-member to walk their friend outside and the staff-member will feel obliged to do so because they usually vouched for the person earlier on.

TIP #77

Know the law concerning evictions and use it as the bad guy.

Example 1 - You say, "Sorry sir, I hate to do this, but unfortunately the bar manager has asked me to move you on for the night." When they ask why, you state that, under the law of your State, if someone is showing signs of intoxication then you are legally obligated to ask them to leave and, unfortunately, the bar manager has made the decision that they are showing those signs.

Example 2 - You have asked the person numerous times to leave and they are refusing. You then advise that you will call the police if necessary who can issue a fine of up to $2,000 (or whatever it is in your State). The more specific you are on the fine they can receive, the more likely they are to believe you.

Example 3 - An AIP demands that they have the right to finish their drink and then drags it out over the next half an hour. In this case it can be easier to arrange with management beforehand to get the person a refund so you can take their drink off them, rather than having to babysit them for half an hour waiting for their drink to finish. When they say they have the 'right' to be on the premises, you can also clarify their legal position and use the opportunity to gain some standing in their eyes, by advising them that they actually only have a 'licence' to remain on the premises which can be revoked by management at any time and that you represent management. A statement of this nature will be too confusing in the AIP's intoxicated state and thus give you the opportunity to move them on while they try to figure out what you said.

TIP #78

When breaking up a confrontation, I often **encourage the more timid patron to leave** the area because, despite all their hot air, they do not actually want to be there, so it is easier to get them to leave than the more aggressive AIP. As discussed further in the next Tip, I then reapproach the aggressive AIP and evict them in a manner which still appears to be on their side.

Example - An underworld connected guy (Guy 1) was in the club one night and hitting on another guy's (Guy 2) girlfriend. Guy 2 clearly felt uncomfortable in this situation, but stood up to Guy 1 and his gang. Having dealt with Guy 1 many times, I knew Guy 2 did not stand a chance against him and if he did not back down quickly there would be hell to pay. I approached Guy 2 and let him know that Guy 1 was heavily connected so he should drop his moral high ground and leave the club. Guy 2 predictably refused arguing that he could take them all on, etc. to appear macho to his girlfriend, so I told him he was welcome to stay, but that I could not guarantee what would happen next. As the matter began to escalate, I then focused my attention on Guy 2's girlfriend and acted panicky saying she needed to get her boyfriend out of the club. The girlfriend then got Guy 2 out of the club which enabled him to save face to Guy 1 because he was only leaving because his "girlfriend and the bouncers were making him."

TIP #79

When breaking up a fight it is useful to initially **make it look as though you are on the more aggressive patron's side** to keep them in check and move the weaker person away. Once they are broken up, the weaker person can be smoothed over by apologizing and saying you had the wrong facts and then you can re-approach the more aggressive patron and say that, unfortunately the manager saw the event and you now have no choice but to evict them (good guy/bad guy).

Example 1 - I once diffused a fight by grabbing the victim by the shoulder and forcing him up the road while shouting at him. This created the apparency that I was on the aggressor group's side even though I was actually saving the victim, and once out of sight of the aggressor group I led the victim to the safest exit path and he profusely thanked me for helping him.

Example 2 - Again, I once diffused a fight by initially evicting the weaker people involved and joking around with the aggressors. I then returned a few minutes later and told the aggressors in a rushed, urgent manner that the police were coming inside in a minute so they better get out quickly. I then showed them where the back door was, and they left thanking me for being such a great bouncer.

TIP #80

When a dispute arises in a venue it is useful to **impose yourself in the middle of the two or more AIPs** and insist they quietly take it outside. Although they will no doubt abuse you at first, as you continue to interrupt their communication with each other, they will get more and more annoyed at you and eventually end up walking outside, at which point you can man up the front door to prevent them coming back in until the dispute is completely over.

TIP #81

When people initially start verbally abusing each other but it has not yet turned physical, quickly intervene and give them the choice to either each relocate to another part of the venue or they will need to leave. By giving them a choice they are forced to **choose the lesser of the two evils**, which still resolves the situation (win/win).

TIP #82

Give the AIP hope of being able to enter the venue later on if they leave now. When you finally get the AIP into a state of mind of agreeing to leave, nine times out of ten you will be asked whether they can come back inside later on once they have drunk some water. Don't provide a definitive answer to this, but rather encourage them to go and have something to eat with some water and try again in an hour and emphasize the <u>actual time</u> you want them to come back, otherwise they will just rock up again five minutes later with a big hopeful grin on their face. Don't commit to letting them back in if they leave now but just give them the hope to get them onside and then reassess the situation when they return. Often they will either not come back at all and if they do, after an hour out in the cold with food and water, they will be less intoxicated and ready to continue having a good night. If they come back and the front doorman thinks they are still too intoxicated, then they won't let them in and you can just avoid being around the front door if the AIP starts whining and insisting that you said they could come back in.

TIP #83

When I have already given several warnings and the AIP and their friends are basically challenging me to physically evict them, I will often **hang around intruding on their conversation** and even sit down at their table continuously interrupting them with my boring conversation. This takes a bit of nerve at first but can be very effective as nobody likes to have their communication continuously cut off and in my experience the less confrontational people in the group, such as the AIP's girlfriend, will give in first and encourage the rest of the group to leave.

TIP #84

When an AIP is misbehaving and they will not listen to you because they feel that as a bouncer you are in some way below them, **find somebody they will listen to who can help with the eviction.**

Example 1 - I once used this against a young lawyer who was playing up by finding an older lawyer I knew in the bar to walk up and ask the young man's name, while I was stood there to persuade him to pull his head in.

Example 2 - Another time a young man was trying to start a fight at a private party, so I approached an older looking women of a similar cultural background to the man which was known for their high value on respect for women and one's elders, and discussed with her how appalling this young man's behavior was. She eventually walked over, gave him a smack over the head, walked him outside herself and proceeded to strip him down for the next 15 minutes. Wonderful tactic!

TIP #85

Have a period(s) in the night when **eviction sweeps** are done. Get together the largest crowd controllers and even the manager and move through with <u>intention</u> and urgency telling anyone you want out to quickly finish up and exit the venue. When they ask why, tell them something along the lines that you just found out Liquor Licensing is at the venue down the road and heading towards your venue so the manager has instructed you to remove anybody who is even borderline intoxicated. Apologize to them and say that once you have the all clear they might be able to get back in after some water, etc. As they see lots of people being evicted at the same time, it will add credibility to your story and encourage them to leave quickly. Once they are out, you can leave it up to the front doorman whether or not to let them back inside and he can plead ignorance to your saying you might let them back in.

TIP #86

There are multiple ways to **use your environment** to gain leverage during evictions depending on the situation. Some of which include:

1. If the AIP is standing with their **girlfriend, children, work colleagues**, etc. you can utilize them in your eviction routine by saying e.g. "Come on buddy, I don't want to do this in front of your children, so best that you come out quietly;"

2. Asking the AIP's name and telling them that a **taxi is waiting** for them outside. When they question who ordered it, just act ignorant and say they better come outside and chat to the driver themself. When they come outside and find there is no taxi (unless there is e.g. A taxi rank nearby), just play dumb as though the taxi has now left and encourage them to head home for the night. When they protest that you are, 'kicking them out', just keep them occupied in conversation for a while and arrange for somebody to call a taxi. It is surprising how often this works, but when they are heavily

intoxicated and you run through this routine with <u>intention</u>, the AIP will almost always go along with it;

3. Females in particular can be very difficult to evict because they know you will be reluctant to touch them physically because of the repercussions of being accused of sexual assault, picking on a little girl and so on. Therefore, I often resort to other tactics such as a **random ID check** which I do spontaneously and without any warning that I intend to evict them. Once they show me their ID, I ask them to follow me for a moment and then just walk outside with <u>intention</u> as though I am doing something important. As they need their ID they will usually follow me, at which point I advise them that I am unable to let them back inside;

4. Let the person know you have **personal details** such as the name and contact details of the person who arranged the party; you still have their credit card at the front desk; you know where they work [if you can find that out]; if your venue has an ID scanner, remind them that you have a copy of their ID; you will send a photo of them to other venues in the area to ensure they get blacklisted from local venues in the future, etc....the list is endless;

5. As mentioned at Tip #79, telling the aggressor that the **police are coming** in to look for them and making it look as though you are helping them out is also an effective use of your environment to encourage them to leave the venue;

6. Walk up to the guy you want out, ask their name and pretend they are the person you are looking for and say that there is a **girl outside whom you are not letting in** because the venue is at capacity, or some other reason, but she said that that guy could vouch for her. Every guy loves to play the hero, so when they come outside to get the girl, don't let them back in on the ground of intoxication and run through the routine as outlined in Tip #73 now that you have gained leverage over them by getting them outside;

7. If a group of AIPs are getting on somebody's nerves, you could approach the girlfriends of the AIPs, or the weaker looking AIPs and

exaggerate the situation by stressing they have messed with the wrong person and based on past experience you think they should leave the venue. As you let it sizzle for a moment and look nervous and panicky, the girlfriends or weaker AIPs will often then encourage the rest of the group to leave and the AIPs in the group will save face because their friends are making them leave instead of them leaving 'because they are scared', etc.

8. If you have a dodgy group of AIPs in the venue whom you suspect are involved with drugs, you could even **contact the police** who are then obliged to attend. The police will then usually take the group outside to search them and once they try to get back inside, you can refuse them entry while the police are still hovering around.

TIP #87

The eviction of groups of AIPs is best accomplished by **focusing on one member of the group** whom the group's activity centres around to encourage the whole group to leave. It is best to try and isolate that person by eg. waiting for them to go to the toilet or outside for a cigarette. Then encourage that person to come outside using one of the tricks outlined in the last Tip and tell the front doorman not to let them back inside. The rest of the group can then be brought outside by letting the leader of the group know that their friend is unable to come back in due to their being over intoxicated. The group can also be encouraged to come outside quickly with a diversion such as telling them that there is a dodgy guy outside hassling their friend, which will usually cause them to run outside. Once they are outside, you have gained significant leverage over them as discussed at TIP #73 and can use that to gain their compliance to leave with a win/win scenario such as allowing one of them back inside for a moment to grab their stuff, finish their drink, grab their friend, etc.

TIP #88

When evicting somebody you can soften the blow by stating that you are **not banning them forever** but just for that night and they are welcome to come back the following night. You can even provide them with discount vouchers for the following night or tell them to drop your name to the doorman at another venue to encourage them to leave. This usually does no harm because if they are too intoxicated they probably won't remember your name anyway, and the doorman at your venue and the venue you referred them too, still have discretion whether or not to let them in.

You can even offer to buy them a drink if they come back the following day, but naturally schedule this offer to a time when you are not working, to avoid an awkward moment when some dude rocks up asking you to buy him a drink.

TIP #89

Point out cameras. If the AIP refuses to leave the venue willingly and you perceive they may become aggressive, it is wise to advise them that there are multiple cameras inside the venue and that it would therefore be wise for them to leave with as little fuss as possible.

As a side note, when evicting AIPs, particularly of the female breed, you should do your best to move them within view of the video camera, to protect yourself from allegations of assault/sexual assault as this allegation is practically a nightly experience in the world of evictions.

TIP #90

When moving in to do the eviction it is wise to surround the AIP in a **triangle formation**, with one person doing the talking at the front and the other two at the back to assist physically if necessary. This formation should be continued for the duration of the eviction, with the talking crowd controller at the front leading the way out and the two at the back watching the back of the leading crowd controller and holding the AIP's arms if necessary.

A pre-arranged signal such as scratching one's nose should also be used by a security team when conducting evictions so the team knows at what stage to become physical.

TIP #91

If you are teamed up with inexperienced crowd controllers, you can still utilize them by getting them to stand behind the AIP in the case of an eviction, to create the **psychological effect that they are surrounded**, even though you know that these crowd controllers would be useless in the event that anything actually happened. You can also utilize these types of crowd controllers to walk ahead of the path of the eviction and to the exit door, to remove bottles and other potential weapons from the area. They can also be useful for occupying the AIP's friends with conversation and just generally distracting them so you can move in to do the eviction.

TIP #92

When involved in an eviction **be highly alert as to how bystanders perceive you**. Because you are the 'bouncer', bystanders automatically presume you are more skilled in martial arts and stronger than the AIP you are evicting and so the slightest aggression could be exaggerated in their eyes and you must be mindful of the effect it will have if the crowd turns against you. It is wise to always smile and have your hands in an open position in front of you making it appear you are not aggressive, yet still keeping your hands up in case you are attacked.

TIP #93

Usually the front doorman is the most experienced crowd controller in the team and will come inside to do the eviction. Once the eviction is complete it is therefore useful to **rotate that front doorman** inside, to reduce the tension of having him outside with the AIPs who have just been evicted. Just put the second most experienced person on the front door, who can then calm the situation using eg. the good guy/bad guy approach.

TIP #94

Be aware of your environment as you do an eviction. I have lost count of the amount of times the bollards out front of the venue have been picked up and used as weapons after an eviction, because they were not heavy enough and the front doorman was not fast enough to move the bollards inside before the AIPs were evicted. Also, watch for glass bottles and glasses out front which could very quickly be turned into weapons after an eviction.

TIP #95

When evicting feuding parties, always evict them out **different exits** or allow them to leave with their friends close by so they don't get nailed as they depart.

TIP #96

If the eviction becomes physical, you should still **continue to talk** to the AIP to reassure them that you are not going to hurt them if they don't resist you. Often they are only pretending to resist you to save face in front of the girls in the room, etc. but will actually walk quite willingly with you if they do not feel you are a threat to them. As you walk them out of the venue, you should continuously repeat phrases such as, "Just this way, buddy," "I am not here to fight you," "I am just doing my job." Then, as the eviction comes to an end let them know that you are now going to release them and again repeat that you are, "Not here to fight them," or "The police are just around the corner," etc. to cool them down before physically letting them go.

TIP #97

Although this text does not seek to cover the physical aspect of evictions, it is recommended that you at least do a **basic course on wrist locks** and general self-defense. Many security training companies offer such courses which go for one or more days and can be very useful for those who lack a martial arts background.

The law in most countries states that the force used for evictions must be, "reasonable and necessary" which involves the following force continuum, which is a scale of how much force can be used by a crowd controller to overcome oppositional force depending on how their subject is responding:

1. Physical presence;

2. Verbal commands;

3. Empty-hand submission techniques;

4. Intermediate weapons (closed-fist punches, kicks, batons, etc.); and

5. Lethal force.

Because of my background as a lawyer, I am reluctant to discuss in more detail what use of force is appropriate to specific situations because of the risk that my commentary will be relied on as legal advice. However, I do encourage you to explore this issue further and note that for those with a martial arts background, be aware that this may count against you in the eyes of the Court if ever you are charged by the police or sued for assault, because it is assumed you will have had the training to cause less damage than you may have caused.

It is my intention to produce a further text at a later date on the physical techniques found most useful in crowd control, but in the meantime there are plenty of existing resources out there on this subject.

TIP #98

Always back your fellow crowd controller's call. There is nothing worse than two crowd controllers saying different things and confusing the poor AIP's already intoxicated mind and, further, they will play on this weakness once detecting it. If this means evicting someone unjustly then do so, but then let them back in once you have clarified the situation better.

TIP #99

After an eviction or an AIP leaves on their own free will and you do not want them back in the venue, ensure you **communicate the eviction to the front doorman.** Kicking out an AIP the first time is hard enough and once they get back in, they will not want to leave! Communicate they have been 'cut off' with a subtle signal such as a hand swipe of your neck.

TIP #100

After an eviction, try to **redirect the AIP's attention** to encourage them to move on for the night.

Example 1 - It is a cold night and the AIP is just hanging around talking to you in an attempt to smooth you over so you let them back inside. Try to keep the conversation to a minimum so they do not get too comfortable, and talk about how you can't wait to get a kebab from down the road and get home to your warm bed. Keep talking about how cold you are and rub your hands together or talk about how the AIP is more likely to meet girls at a venue down the road, etc. to help plant the seed in their mind that they should move on.

The same tactic can be used when clearing the venue at the end of the night, so they do not feel that their night is coming to an end if they leave the venue.

Example 2 - I once had to close down a private party at midnight because the liquor licence had expired. The majority of guests were very intoxicated and fully intent on continuing their party. I therefore gave them directions to the nearest nightclubs which were still open and even typed the directions into their phones to get them onside and subtly guided them out of the party with <u>*intention*</u>*, which worked like a charm.*

6 LAST DRINKS

TIP #101

Never stop learning and do not give up. It may be just a night job but in my experience the art of crowd control has always presented numerous opportunities to strengthen your character and grow as a person. Always push your comfort zone and recognize that you can do better.

Listen to more experienced crowd controllers. The finer details of how to be a professional crowd controller can only be learned in the field through practice and trial and error to find what works for you. Most experienced crowd controllers are more than happy to teach those who are eager to learn and will involve you in more of the confronting situations if they can see that you are willing to do it their way and learn from them.

There will be times in crowd control when you find yourself hiding in the toilets wondering why the hell you ever took on this job. Read this book again, see if there are any concepts you did not fully grasp and figure out what you can do better. If you are still not sure, sort out a more experienced and approachable crowd controller and see if they have any pet techniques that could help you.

Remember:

"Men succeed when they realize that their failures are the preparation for their victories." - Ralph Waldo Emerson

BULK ORDERS

If you are a security company, security training provider or run an entertainment venue requiring security and wish to order bulk copies of this book, I welcome your email on DarrenLeeAuthor@gmail.com to discuss pricing.

Made in the USA
Middletown, DE
19 May 2015